IF FOUND, THIS JOURNAL BELONGS TO:

_____

INSERT NAME

Stylish Writing Center

— WRITE & SLAY —

Greetings,

Thank you for taking that step to purchase this gratitude, self-care, and self-reflection journal. I realize you had many options and chose this one.

This guided journal aims to help you decide what to write while reflecting upon your day. It's okay to take a few minutes to think about the thoughts and emotions that guided your actions. Taking time to acknowledge this leads to self-awareness and gives insight into what you are doing well and where adjustments can be made in your daily life.

Moreover, this journal helps you see the goodness around you and within you.

Being mindful that there is something to always be thankful for will keep you aware of goodness and kindheartedness.

Take your time as you reflect and write in this journal. You'll see just how much of a difference acknowledging your thoughts, feelings, and emotions (and being thankful) will make in your life. But, of course, it won't hurt to incorporate a little self-care too!

Kinyatta

"GRATITUDE IS THE INWARD FEELING OF KINDNESS RECEIVED. THANKFULNESS IS THE NATURAL IMPULSE TO EXPRESS THAT FEELING."

~Henry Van Dyke

GRATITUDE CHECKLIST

- ☐ I am thankful for my mind, body and spirit

- ☐ I am thankful for how I generate income and financial independence

- ☐ I am thankful for the relationships I have with family members and friends

- ☐ I am thankful for a companion, spouse, or significant other to share my life with

- ☐ I am thankful for my creativity and extraordinary talents

- ☐ I am thankful for others who perform services (dry cleaners, Uber drivers, etc.) that add convenience to my life

- ☐ I am thankful for the lessons I learn daily

- ☐ I am thankful for the autonomy to make critical life decisions

- ☐ I am thankful for having a reason to smile every day

- ☐ I am thankful for those who trust and believe in me

7-DAYS OF GRATITUDE

SUNDAY
"Learn to be thankful for what you already have as you pursue all that you want." ~Jim Rohn

MONDAY
"This is a wonderful day. I've never seen this one before." ~Maya Angelou

TUESDAY
"If a fella isn't thankful for what he's got, he's not going to be thankful for what he's going to get." ~Frank A. Clark

WEDNESDAY
"When you are grateful, fear disappears and abundance appears." ~Tony Robbins

THURSDAY
"Thanks for loving me despite my flaws." ~UNKNOWN

FRIDAY
"When I started counting my blessings, my whole life turned around." ~Willie Nelson

SATURDAY
"A thankful heart is not only the greatest virtue, but the parent of all other virtues." ~Cicero

WHAT KIND OF MAN ARE YOU?
DESCRIBE YOURSELF IN 30 WORDS.

1. _____
2. _____
3. _____
4. _____
5. _____
6. _____
7. _____
8. _____
9. _____
10. _____
11. _____
12. _____
13. _____
14. _____
15. _____
16. _____
17. _____
18. _____
19. _____
20. _____
21. _____
22. _____
23. _____
24. _____
25. _____
26. _____
27. _____
28. _____
29. _____
30. _____

"EMOTIONS HAVE NO GENDER.
DON'T LOCK YOURS IN THE
DARK."

~Self Esteem Team

THOUGHTS ABOUT ENTREPRENEURSHIP/ CAREER/EDUCATION...

THOUGHTS ABOUT ENTREPRENEURSHIP/ CAREER/EDUCATION...

THOUGHTS ABOUT ENTREPRENEURSHIP/ CAREER/EDUCATION...

THOUGHTS ABOUT MY FAMILY & CHILDHOOD...

THOUGHTS ABOUT MY FAMILY & CHILDHOOD...

_____

_____

_____

_____

_____

_____

_____

_____

_____

_____

_____

_____

_____

_____

_____

_____

_____

_____

_____

_____

_____

THOUGHTS ABOUT MY FAMILY & CHILDHOOD...

_____

_____

_____

_____

_____

_____

_____

_____

_____

_____

_____

_____

_____

_____

_____

_____

_____

_____

_____

_____

_____

THOUGHTS ABOUT MY COMPANION/ SIGNIFICANT OTHER/LIFE PARTNER AND MARRIAGE...

_____

_____

_____

_____

_____

_____

_____

_____

_____

_____

_____

_____

_____

_____

_____

_____

_____

_____

_____

THOUGHTS ABOUT MY COMPANION/ SIGNIFICANT OTHER/LIFE PARTNER AND MARRIAGE...

_____

_____

_____

_____

_____

_____

_____

_____

_____

_____

_____

_____

_____

_____

_____

_____

_____

_____

_____

THOUGHTS ABOUT MY COMPANION/ SIGNIFICANT OTHER/LIFE PARTNER AND MARRIAGE...

_____

_____

_____

_____

_____

_____

_____

_____

_____

_____

_____

_____

_____

_____

_____

_____

_____

_____

_____

_____

_____

THOUGHTS ABOUT RAISING CHILDREN AND/ OR STARTING A FAMILY...

_____

_____

_____

_____

_____

_____

_____

_____

_____

_____

_____

_____

_____

_____

_____

_____

_____

_____

_____

THOUGHTS ABOUT RAISING CHILDREN AND/ OR STARTING A FAMILY...

_____

_____

_____

_____

_____

_____

_____

_____

_____

_____

_____

_____

_____

_____

_____

_____

_____

_____

_____

THOUGHTS ABOUT RAISING CHILDREN AND/ OR STARTING A FAMILY...

_____

_____

_____

_____

_____

_____

_____

_____

_____

_____

_____

_____

_____

_____

_____

_____

_____

_____

THOUGHTS ABOUT MY FRIENDS...

THOUGHTS ABOUT MY FRIENDS...

_____

_____

_____

_____

_____

_____

_____

_____

_____

_____

_____

_____

_____

_____

_____

_____

_____

_____

_____

_____

_____

_____

THOUGHTS ABOUT MY FRIENDS...

I'M FRUSTRATED BY...

I'M FRUSTRATED BY...

_____

_____

_____

_____

_____

_____

_____

_____

_____

_____

_____

_____

_____

_____

_____

_____

_____

_____

_____

_____

_____

_____

I'M FRUSTRATED BY...

_____

_____

_____

_____

_____

_____

_____

_____

_____

_____

_____

_____

_____

_____

_____

_____

_____

_____

_____

_____

LEAVING A LEGACY

Are you living your life in the way that you want to be remembered?

_____

_____

_____

What would you change?

_____

_____

_____

What will you continue doing?

_____

_____

_____

Whose lives have you touched?

_____

_____

_____

"WHEN YOU RECOVER OR
DISCOVER SOMETHING THAT
NOURISHES YOUR SOUL AND
BRINGS JOY, CARE ENOUGH
ABOUT YOURSELF TO MAKE
ROOM FOR IT IN YOUR LIFE."

~Jean Shinoda Bolen

30 DAYS OF SELF-CARE

Hold yourself accountable for your well-being by committing to 30-days of self-care activities.

DATE	SELF-CARE ACTIVITY	AFTER COMPLETING THIS ACTIVITY, I FELT...

60-DAYS OF SELF-REFLECTIONS

Date: /   /

When I need support, I can count on...	**Today I Feel:**
	☐ Optimistic
I felt inspired when...	☐ Happy
	☐ Uneasy
	☐ Frustrated
I felt happiest when...	☐ Lonely
	☐ Angry
	☐ Tired

I am grateful for...

I felt disrespected/stressed when...

I spoke up when...

I could have done this better...

I know I'm the "man" when...

This was hard but I overcame it by...

I will relax and indulge in self-care today by...

This is what I will remember most about today:

60-DAYS OF SELF-REFLECTIONS

Date: /   /

	Today I Feel:
When I need support, I can count on...	☐ Optimistic
	☐ Happy
I felt inspired when...	☐ Uneasy
	☐ Frustrated
	☐ Lonely
I felt happiest when...	☐ Angry
	☐ Tired

I am grateful for...

I felt disrespected/stressed when...

I spoke up when...

I could have done this better...

I know I'm the "man" when...

This was hard but I overcame it by...

I will relax and indulge in self-care today by...

This is what I will remember most about today:

60-DAYS OF SELF-REFLECTIONS

Date: /   /

When I need support, I can count on...	**Today I Feel:**
	☐ Optimistic
I felt inspired when...	☐ Happy
	☐ Uneasy
	☐ Frustrated
I felt happiest when...	☐ Lonely
	☐ Angry
	☐ Tired

I am grateful for...

I felt disrespected/stressed when...

I spoke up when...

I could have done this better...

I know I'm the "man" when...

This was hard but I overcame it by...

I will relax and indulge in self-care today by...

This is what I will remember most about today:

60-DAYS OF SELF-REFLECTIONS

Date: /   /

When I need support, I can count on...	**Today I Feel:**
	☐ Optimistic
	☐ Happy
I felt inspired when...	☐ Uneasy
	☐ Frustrated
	☐ Lonely
I felt happiest when...	☐ Angry
	☐ Tired

I am grateful for...

I felt disrespected/stressed when...

I spoke up when...

I could have done this better...

I know I'm the "man" when...

This was hard but I overcame it by...

I will relax and indulge in self-care today by...

This is what I will remember most about today:

60-DAYS OF SELF-REFLECTIONS

Date: /   /

When I need support, I can count on...	**Today I Feel:**
	☐ Optimistic
	☐ Happy
I felt inspired when...	☐ Uneasy
	☐ Frustrated
	☐ Lonely
I felt happiest when...	☐ Angry
	☐ Tired

I am grateful for...

I felt disrespected/stressed when...

I spoke up when...

I could have done this better...

I know I'm the "man" when...

This was hard but I overcame it by...

I will relax and indulge in self-care today by...

This is what I will remember most about today:

60-DAYS OF SELF-REFLECTIONS

Date: /   /

When I need support, I can count on...	**Today I Feel:**
	☐ Optimistic
	☐ Happy
I felt inspired when...	☐ Uneasy
	☐ Frustrated
	☐ Lonely
I felt happiest when...	☐ Angry
	☐ Tired

I am grateful for...

I felt disrespected/stressed when...

I spoke up when...

I could have done this better...

I know I'm the "man" when...

This was hard but I overcame it by...

I will relax and indulge in self-care today by...

This is what I will remember most about today:

60-DAYS OF SELF-REFLECTIONS

Date: /   /

When I need support, I can count on...	Today I Feel:
	☐ Optimistic
I felt inspired when...	☐ Happy
	☐ Uneasy
	☐ Frustrated
I felt happiest when...	☐ Lonely
	☐ Angry
	☐ Tired

I am grateful for...

I felt disrespected/stressed when...

I spoke up when...

I could have done this better...

I know I'm the "man" when...

This was hard but I overcame it by...

I will relax and indulge in self-care today by...

This is what I will remember most about today:

60-DAYS OF SELF-REFLECTIONS

Date: /   /

When I need support, I can count on...	**Today I Feel:**
	☐ Optimistic
	☐ Happy
I felt inspired when...	☐ Uneasy
	☐ Frustrated
	☐ Lonely
I felt happiest when...	☐ Angry
	☐ Tired

I am grateful for...

I felt disrespected/stressed when...

I spoke up when...

I could have done this better...

I know I'm the "man" when...

This was hard but I overcame it by...

I will relax and indulge in self-care today by...

This is what I will remember most about today:

60-DAYS OF SELF-REFLECTIONS

Date: /   /

When I need support, I can count on...	**Today I Feel:**
	☐ Optimistic
I felt inspired when...	☐ Happy
	☐ Uneasy
	☐ Frustrated
I felt happiest when...	☐ Lonely
	☐ Angry
	☐ Tired

I am grateful for...

I felt disrespected/stressed when...

I spoke up when...

I could have done this better...

I know I'm the "man" when...

This was hard but I overcame it by...

I will relax and indulge in self-care today by...

This is what I will remember most about today:

60-DAYS OF SELF-REFLECTIONS

Date: /   /

When I need support, I can count on...	**Today I Feel:**
	☐ Optimistic
	☐ Happy
I felt inspired when...	☐ Uneasy
	☐ Frustrated
	☐ Lonely
I felt happiest when...	☐ Angry
	☐ Tired

I am grateful for...

I felt disrespected/stressed when...

I spoke up when...

I could have done this better...

I know I'm the "man" when...

This was hard but I overcame it by...

I will relax and indulge in self-care today by...

This is what I will remember most about today:

60-DAYS OF SELF-REFLECTIONS

Date: /   /

When I need support, I can count on...	**Today I Feel:**
	☐ Optimistic
I felt inspired when...	☐ Happy
	☐ Uneasy
	☐ Frustrated
I felt happiest when...	☐ Lonely
	☐ Angry
	☐ Tired

I am grateful for...

I felt disrespected/stressed when...

I spoke up when...

I could have done this better...

I know I'm the "man" when...

This was hard but I overcame it by...

I will relax and indulge in self-care today by...

This is what I will remember most about today:

60-DAYS OF SELF-REFLECTIONS

Date: /   /

When I need support, I can count on...	**Today I Feel:**
	☐ Optimistic
	☐ Happy
I felt inspired when...	☐ Uneasy
	☐ Frustrated
	☐ Lonely
I felt happiest when...	☐ Angry
	☐ Tired

I am grateful for...

I felt disrespected/stressed when...

I spoke up when...

I could have done this better...

I know I'm the "man" when...

This was hard but I overcame it by...

I will relax and indulge in self-care today by...

This is what I will remember most about today:

60-DAYS OF SELF-REFLECTIONS

Date: /   /

When I need support, I can count on...	**Today I Feel:**
	☐ Optimistic
I felt inspired when...	☐ Happy
	☐ Uneasy
	☐ Frustrated
I felt happiest when...	☐ Lonely
	☐ Angry
	☐ Tired

I am grateful for...

I felt disrespected/stressed when...

I spoke up when...

I could have done this better...

I know I'm the "man" when...

This was hard but I overcame it by...

I will relax and indulge in self-care today by...

This is what I will remember most about today:

60-DAYS OF SELF-REFLECTIONS

Date: /   /

When I need support, I can count on...	**Today I Feel:**
	☐ Optimistic
	☐ Happy
I felt inspired when...	☐ Uneasy
	☐ Frustrated
	☐ Lonely
I felt happiest when...	☐ Angry
	☐ Tired

I am grateful for...

I felt disrespected/stressed when...

I spoke up when...

I could have done this better...

I know I'm the "man" when...

This was hard but I overcame it by...

I will relax and indulge in self-care today by...

This is what I will remember most about today:

60-DAYS OF SELF-REFLECTIONS

Date: /   /

When I need support, I can count on...	**Today I Feel:** ☐ Optimistic ☐ Happy ☐ Uneasy ☐ Frustrated ☐ Lonely ☐ Angry ☐ Tired
I felt inspired when...	
I felt happiest when...	

I am grateful for...

I felt disrespected/stressed when...

I spoke up when...

I could have done this better...

I know I'm the "man" when...

This was hard but I overcame it by...

I will relax and indulge in self-care today by...

This is what I will remember most about today:

60-DAYS OF SELF-REFLECTIONS

Date: /   /

When I need support, I can count on...	**Today I Feel:**
	☐ Optimistic
	☐ Happy
I felt inspired when...	☐ Uneasy
	☐ Frustrated
	☐ Lonely
I felt happiest when...	☐ Angry
	☐ Tired

I am grateful for...

I felt disrespected/stressed when...

I spoke up when...

I could have done this better...

I know I'm the "man" when...

This was hard but I overcame it by...

I will relax and indulge in self-care today by...

This is what I will remember most about today:

60-DAYS OF SELF-REFLECTIONS

Date: /   /

When I need support, I can count on...

Today I Feel:
- ☐ Optimistic
- ☐ Happy
- ☐ Uneasy
- ☐ Frustrated
- ☐ Lonely
- ☐ Angry
- ☐ Tired

I felt inspired when...

I felt happiest when...

I am grateful for...

I felt disrespected/stressed when...

I spoke up when...

I could have done this better...

I know I'm the "man" when...

This was hard but I overcame it by...

I will relax and indulge in self-care today by...

This is what I will remember most about today:

60-DAYS OF SELF-REFLECTIONS

Date: ___ / ___ / ___

	Today I Feel:
When I need support, I can count on...	☐ Optimistic
	☐ Happy
I felt inspired when...	☐ Uneasy
	☐ Frustrated
	☐ Lonely
I felt happiest when...	☐ Angry
	☐ Tired

I am grateful for...

I felt disrespected/stressed when...

I spoke up when...

I could have done this better...

I know I'm the "man" when...

This was hard but I overcame it by...

I will relax and indulge in self-care today by...

This is what I will remember most about today:

60-DAYS OF SELF-REFLECTIONS

Date: /   /

When I need support, I can count on...	**Today I Feel:** ☐ Optimistic ☐ Happy
I felt inspired when...	☐ Uneasy ☐ Frustrated ☐ Lonely
I felt happiest when...	☐ Angry ☐ Tired

I am grateful for...

I felt disrespected/stressed when...

I spoke up when...

I could have done this better...

I know I'm the "man" when...

This was hard but I overcame it by...

I will relax and indulge in self-care today by...

This is what I will remember most about today:

60-DAYS OF SELF-REFLECTIONS

Date: /   /

	Today I Feel:
When I need support, I can count on...	☐ Optimistic
	☐ Happy
I felt inspired when...	☐ Uneasy
	☐ Frustrated
	☐ Lonely
I felt happiest when...	☐ Angry
	☐ Tired

I am grateful for...

I felt disrespected/stressed when...

I spoke up when...

I could have done this better...

I know I'm the "man" when...

This was hard but I overcame it by...

I will relax and indulge in self-care today by...

This is what I will remember most about today:

60-DAYS OF SELF-REFLECTIONS

Date: / /

	Today I Feel:
When I need support, I can count on...	☐ Optimistic
	☐ Happy
I felt inspired when...	☐ Uneasy
	☐ Frustrated
	☐ Lonely
I felt happiest when...	☐ Angry
	☐ Tired

I am grateful for...

I felt disrespected/stressed when...

I spoke up when...

I could have done this better...

I know I'm the "man" when...

This was hard but I overcame it by...

I will relax and indulge in self-care today by...

This is what I will remember most about today:

60-DAYS OF SELF-REFLECTIONS

Date: /   /

When I need support, I can count on...	**Today I Feel:** ☐ Optimistic ☐ Happy
I felt inspired when...	☐ Uneasy ☐ Frustrated ☐ Lonely
I felt happiest when...	☐ Angry ☐ Tired

I am grateful for...

I felt disrespected/stressed when...

I spoke up when...

I could have done this better...

I know I'm the "man" when...

This was hard but I overcame it by...

I will relax and indulge in self-care today by...

This is what I will remember most about today:

60-DAYS OF SELF-REFLECTIONS

Date: /   /

When I need support, I can count on...	**Today I Feel:**
	☐ Optimistic
I felt inspired when...	☐ Happy
	☐ Uneasy
	☐ Frustrated
I felt happiest when...	☐ Lonely
	☐ Angry
	☐ Tired

I am grateful for...

I felt disrespected/stressed when...

I spoke up when...

I could have done this better...

I know I'm the "man" when...

This was hard but I overcame it by...

I will relax and indulge in self-care today by...

This is what I will remember most about today:

60-DAYS OF SELF-REFLECTIONS

Date: /   /

When I need support, I can count on...	**Today I Feel:**
	☐ Optimistic
	☐ Happy
I felt inspired when...	☐ Uneasy
	☐ Frustrated
	☐ Lonely
I felt happiest when...	☐ Angry
	☐ Tired

I am grateful for...

I felt disrespected/stressed when...

I spoke up when...

I could have done this better...

I know I'm the "man" when...

This was hard but I overcame it by...

I will relax and indulge in self-care today by...

This is what I will remember most about today:

60-DAYS OF SELF-REFLECTIONS

Date: /   /

When I need support, I can count on...	**Today I Feel:** ☐ Optimistic ☐ Happy
I felt inspired when...	☐ Uneasy ☐ Frustrated
I felt happiest when...	☐ Lonely ☐ Angry ☐ Tired

I am grateful for...

I felt disrespected/stressed when...

I spoke up when...

I could have done this better...

I know I'm the "man" when...

This was hard but I overcame it by...

I will relax and indulge in self-care today by...

This is what I will remember most about today:

60-DAYS OF SELF-REFLECTIONS

Date: /   /

When I need support, I can count on...	**Today I Feel:**
	☐ Optimistic
	☐ Happy
I felt inspired when...	☐ Uneasy
	☐ Frustrated
	☐ Lonely
I felt happiest when...	☐ Angry
	☐ Tired

I am grateful for...

I felt disrespected/stressed when...

I spoke up when...

I could have done this better...

I know I'm the "man" when...

This was hard but I overcame it by...

I will relax and indulge in self-care today by...

This is what I will remember most about today:

60-DAYS OF SELF-REFLECTIONS

Date: / /

When I need support, I can count on...	**Today I Feel:**
	☐ Optimistic
I felt inspired when...	☐ Happy
	☐ Uneasy
	☐ Frustrated
I felt happiest when...	☐ Lonely
	☐ Angry
	☐ Tired

I am grateful for...

I felt disrespected/stressed when...

I spoke up when...

I could have done this better...

I know I'm the "man" when...

This was hard but I overcame it by...

I will relax and indulge in self-care today by...

This is what I will remember most about today:

60-DAYS OF SELF-REFLECTIONS

Date: /   /

When I need support, I can count on...	**Today I Feel:**
	☐ Optimistic
	☐ Happy
I felt inspired when...	☐ Uneasy
	☐ Frustrated
	☐ Lonely
I felt happiest when...	☐ Angry
	☐ Tired

I am grateful for...

I felt disrespected/stressed when...

I spoke up when...

I could have done this better...

I know I'm the "man" when...

This was hard but I overcame it by...

I will relax and indulge in self-care today by...

This is what I will remember most about today:

60-DAYS OF SELF-REFLECTIONS

Date: /   /

When I need support, I can count on...	**Today I Feel:**
	☐ Optimistic
	☐ Happy
I felt inspired when...	☐ Uneasy
	☐ Frustrated
	☐ Lonely
I felt happiest when...	☐ Angry
	☐ Tired

I am grateful for...

I felt disrespected/stressed when...

I spoke up when...

I could have done this better...

I know I'm the "man" when...

This was hard but I overcame it by...

I will relax and indulge in self-care today by...

This is what I will remember most about today:

60-DAYS OF SELF-REFLECTIONS

Date: /   /

When I need support, I can count on...	**Today I Feel:** ☐ Optimistic ☐ Happy
I felt inspired when...	☐ Uneasy ☐ Frustrated ☐ Lonely
I felt happiest when...	☐ Angry ☐ Tired

I am grateful for...

I felt disrespected/stressed when...

I spoke up when...

I could have done this better...

I know I'm the "man" when...

This was hard but I overcame it by...

I will relax and indulge in self-care today by...

This is what I will remember most about today:

60-DAYS OF SELF-REFLECTIONS

Date: /   /

When I need support, I can count on...

I felt inspired when...

I felt happiest when...

Today I Feel:
- ☐ Optimistic
- ☐ Happy
- ☐ Uneasy
- ☐ Frustrated
- ☐ Lonely
- ☐ Angry
- ☐ Tired

I am grateful for...

I felt disrespected/stressed when...

I spoke up when...

I could have done this better...

I know I'm the "man" when...

This was hard but I overcame it by...

I will relax and indulge in self-care today by...

This is what I will remember most about today:

60-DAYS OF SELF-REFLECTIONS

Date: /   /

When I need support, I can count on...	Today I Feel:
	☐ Optimistic
	☐ Happy
I felt inspired when...	☐ Uneasy
	☐ Frustrated
	☐ Lonely
I felt happiest when...	☐ Angry
	☐ Tired

I am grateful for...

I felt disrespected/stressed when...

I spoke up when...

I could have done this better...

I know I'm the "man" when...

This was hard but I overcame it by...

I will relax and indulge in self-care today by...

This is what I will remember most about today:

60-DAYS OF SELF-REFLECTIONS

Date: /   /

When I need support, I can count on...

Today I Feel:
- ☐ Optimistic
- ☐ Happy
- ☐ Uneasy
- ☐ Frustrated
- ☐ Lonely
- ☐ Angry
- ☐ Tired

I felt inspired when...

I felt happiest when...

I am grateful for...

I felt disrespected/stressed when...

I spoke up when...

I could have done this better...

I know I'm the "man" when...

This was hard but I overcame it by...

I will relax and indulge in self-care today by...

This is what I will remember most about today:

60-DAYS OF SELF-REFLECTIONS

Date: /   /

When I need support, I can count on...	**Today I Feel:**
	☐ Optimistic
	☐ Happy
I felt inspired when...	☐ Uneasy
	☐ Frustrated
	☐ Lonely
I felt happiest when...	☐ Angry
	☐ Tired

I am grateful for...

I felt disrespected/stressed when...

I spoke up when...

I could have done this better...

I know I'm the "man" when...

This was hard but I overcame it by...

I will relax and indulge in self-care today by...

This is what I will remember most about today:

60-DAYS OF SELF-REFLECTIONS

Date: /   /

When I need support, I can count on...	**Today I Feel:**
	☐ Optimistic
I felt inspired when...	☐ Happy
	☐ Uneasy
	☐ Frustrated
I felt happiest when...	☐ Lonely
	☐ Angry
	☐ Tired

I am grateful for...

I felt disrespected/stressed when...

I spoke up when...

I could have done this better...

I know I'm the "man" when...

This was hard but I overcame it by...

I will relax and indulge in self-care today by...

This is what I will remember most about today:

60-DAYS OF SELF-REFLECTIONS

Date: /   /

When I need support, I can count on...	**Today I Feel:**
	☐ Optimistic
	☐ Happy
I felt inspired when...	☐ Uneasy
	☐ Frustrated
	☐ Lonely
I felt happiest when...	☐ Angry
	☐ Tired

I am grateful for...

I felt disrespected/stressed when...

I spoke up when...

I could have done this better...

I know I'm the "man" when...

This was hard but I overcame it by...

I will relax and indulge in self-care today by...

This is what I will remember most about today:

60-DAYS OF SELF-REFLECTIONS

Date: /   /

	Today I Feel:
When I need support, I can count on...	☐ Optimistic
	☐ Happy
I felt inspired when...	☐ Uneasy
	☐ Frustrated
	☐ Lonely
I felt happiest when...	☐ Angry
	☐ Tired

I am grateful for...

I felt disrespected/stressed when...

I spoke up when...

I could have done this better...

I know I'm the "man" when...

This was hard but I overcame it by...

I will relax and indulge in self-care today by...

This is what I will remember most about today:

60-DAYS OF SELF-REFLECTIONS

Date: /   /

When I need support, I can count on...	**Today I Feel:**
	☐ Optimistic
	☐ Happy
I felt inspired when...	☐ Uneasy
	☐ Frustrated
	☐ Lonely
I felt happiest when...	☐ Angry
	☐ Tired

I am grateful for...

I felt disrespected/stressed when...

I spoke up when...

I could have done this better...

I know I'm the "man" when...

This was hard but I overcame it by...

I will relax and indulge in self-care today by...

This is what I will remember most about today:

60-DAYS OF SELF-REFLECTIONS

Date: /   /

When I need support, I can count on...	**Today I Feel:**
	☐ Optimistic
I felt inspired when...	☐ Happy
	☐ Uneasy
	☐ Frustrated
I felt happiest when...	☐ Lonely
	☐ Angry
	☐ Tired

I am grateful for...

I felt disrespected/stressed when...

I spoke up when...

I could have done this better...

I know I'm the "man" when...

This was hard but I overcame it by...

I will relax and indulge in self-care today by...

This is what I will remember most about today:

60-DAYS OF SELF-REFLECTIONS

Date: /   /

When I need support, I can count on...	**Today I Feel:**
	☐ Optimistic
	☐ Happy
I felt inspired when...	☐ Uneasy
	☐ Frustrated
	☐ Lonely
I felt happiest when...	☐ Angry
	☐ Tired

I am grateful for...

I felt disrespected/stressed when...

I spoke up when...

I could have done this better...

I know I'm the "man" when...

This was hard but I overcame it by...

I will relax and indulge in self-care today by...

This is what I will remember most about today:

60-DAYS OF SELF-REFLECTIONS

Date: /   /

When I need support, I can count on...

I felt inspired when...

I felt happiest when...

Today I Feel:
- ☐ Optimistic
- ☐ Happy
- ☐ Uneasy
- ☐ Frustrated
- ☐ Lonely
- ☐ Angry
- ☐ Tired

I am grateful for...

I felt disrespected/stressed when...

I spoke up when...

I could have done this better...

I know I'm the "man" when...

This was hard but I overcame it by...

I will relax and indulge in self-care today by...

This is what I will remember most about today:

60-DAYS OF SELF-REFLECTIONS

Date: /   /

When I need support, I can count on...	**Today I Feel:**
	☐ Optimistic
	☐ Happy
I felt inspired when...	☐ Uneasy
	☐ Frustrated
	☐ Lonely
I felt happiest when...	☐ Angry
	☐ Tired

I am grateful for...

I felt disrespected/stressed when...

I spoke up when...

I could have done this better...

I know I'm the "man" when...

This was hard but I overcame it by...

I will relax and indulge in self-care today by...

This is what I will remember most about today:

60-DAYS OF SELF-REFLECTIONS

Date: / /

When I need support, I can count on...

Today I Feel:
- ☐ Optimistic
- ☐ Happy
- ☐ Uneasy
- ☐ Frustrated
- ☐ Lonely
- ☐ Angry
- ☐ Tired

I felt inspired when...

I felt happiest when...

I am grateful for...

I felt disrespected/stressed when...

I spoke up when...

I could have done this better...

I know I'm the "man" when...

This was hard but I overcame it by...

I will relax and indulge in self-care today by...

This is what I will remember most about today:

60-DAYS OF SELF-REFLECTIONS

Date: /   /

When I need support, I can count on...	**Today I Feel:**
	☐ Optimistic
	☐ Happy
I felt inspired when...	☐ Uneasy
	☐ Frustrated
	☐ Lonely
I felt happiest when...	☐ Angry
	☐ Tired

I am grateful for...

I felt disrespected/stressed when...

I spoke up when...

I could have done this better...

I know I'm the "man" when...

This was hard but I overcame it by...

I will relax and indulge in self-care today by...

This is what I will remember most about today:

60-DAYS OF SELF-REFLECTIONS

Date: /   /

When I need support, I can count on...	**Today I Feel:**
	☐ Optimistic
	☐ Happy
I felt inspired when...	☐ Uneasy
	☐ Frustrated
	☐ Lonely
I felt happiest when...	☐ Angry
	☐ Tired

I am grateful for...

I felt disrespected/stressed when...

I spoke up when...

I could have done this better...

I know I'm the "man" when...

This was hard but I overcame it by...

I will relax and indulge in self-care today by...

This is what I will remember most about today:

60-DAYS OF SELF-REFLECTIONS

Date: /   /

When I need support, I can count on...	**Today I Feel:**
	☐ Optimistic
	☐ Happy
I felt inspired when...	☐ Uneasy
	☐ Frustrated
	☐ Lonely
I felt happiest when...	☐ Angry
	☐ Tired

I am grateful for...

I felt disrespected/stressed when...

I spoke up when...

I could have done this better...

I know I'm the "man" when...

This was hard but I overcame it by...

I will relax and indulge in self-care today by...

This is what I will remember most about today:

60-DAYS OF SELF-REFLECTIONS

Date: /   /

When I need support, I can count on...	**Today I Feel:**
	☐ Optimistic
	☐ Happy
I felt inspired when...	☐ Uneasy
	☐ Frustrated
	☐ Lonely
I felt happiest when...	☐ Angry
	☐ Tired

I am grateful for...

I felt disrespected/stressed when...

I spoke up when...

I could have done this better...

I know I'm the "man" when...

This was hard but I overcame it by...

I will relax and indulge in self-care today by...

This is what I will remember most about today:

60-DAYS OF SELF-REFLECTIONS

Date: /   /

When I need support, I can count on...	**Today I Feel:** ☐ Optimistic ☐ Happy ☐ Uneasy ☐ Frustrated ☐ Lonely ☐ Angry ☐ Tired
I felt inspired when...	
I felt happiest when...	

I am grateful for...

I felt disrespected/stressed when...

I spoke up when...

I could have done this better...

I know I'm the "man" when...

This was hard but I overcame it by...

I will relax and indulge in self-care today by...

This is what I will remember most about today:

60-DAYS OF SELF-REFLECTIONS

Date: / /

	Today I Feel:
When I need support, I can count on...	☐ Optimistic
	☐ Happy
I felt inspired when...	☐ Uneasy
	☐ Frustrated
I felt happiest when...	☐ Lonely
	☐ Angry
	☐ Tired

I am grateful for...

I felt disrespected/stressed when...

I spoke up when...

I could have done this better...

I know I'm the "man" when...

This was hard but I overcame it by...

I will relax and indulge in self-care today by...

This is what I will remember most about today:

60-DAYS OF SELF-REFLECTIONS

Date: /   /

When I need support, I can count on...	**Today I Feel:** ☐ Optimistic ☐ Happy
I felt inspired when...	☐ Uneasy ☐ Frustrated
I felt happiest when...	☐ Lonely ☐ Angry ☐ Tired

I am grateful for...

I felt disrespected/stressed when...

I spoke up when...

I could have done this better...

I know I'm the "man" when...

This was hard but I overcame it by...

I will relax and indulge in self-care today by...

This is what I will remember most about today:

60-DAYS OF SELF-REFLECTIONS

Date: /   /

	Today I Feel:
When I need support, I can count on...	☐ Optimistic
	☐ Happy
I felt inspired when...	☐ Uneasy
	☐ Frustrated
	☐ Lonely
I felt happiest when...	☐ Angry
	☐ Tired

I am grateful for...

I felt disrespected/stressed when...

I spoke up when...

I could have done this better...

I know I'm the "man" when...

This was hard but I overcame it by...

I will relax and indulge in self-care today by...

This is what I will remember most about today:

60-DAYS OF SELF-REFLECTIONS

Date: /   /

When I need support, I can count on...	**Today I Feel:** ☐ Optimistic ☐ Happy
I felt inspired when...	☐ Uneasy ☐ Frustrated ☐ Lonely
I felt happiest when...	☐ Angry ☐ Tired

I am grateful for...

I felt disrespected/stressed when...

I spoke up when...

I could have done this better...

I know I'm the "man" when...

This was hard but I overcame it by...

I will relax and indulge in self-care today by...

This is what I will remember most about today:

60-DAYS OF SELF-REFLECTIONS

Date: /   /

When I need support, I can count on...	**Today I Feel:**
	☐ Optimistic
I felt inspired when...	☐ Happy
	☐ Uneasy
	☐ Frustrated
I felt happiest when...	☐ Lonely
	☐ Angry
	☐ Tired

I am grateful for...

I felt disrespected/stressed when...

I spoke up when...

I could have done this better...

I know I'm the "man" when...

This was hard but I overcame it by...

I will relax and indulge in self-care today by...

This is what I will remember most about today:

60-DAYS OF SELF-REFLECTIONS

Date: /   /

When I need support, I can count on...	**Today I Feel:**
	☐ Optimistic
	☐ Happy
I felt inspired when...	☐ Uneasy
	☐ Frustrated
	☐ Lonely
I felt happiest when...	☐ Angry
	☐ Tired

I am grateful for...

I felt disrespected/stressed when...

I spoke up when...

I could have done this better...

I know I'm the "man" when...

This was hard but I overcame it by...

I will relax and indulge in self-care today by...

This is what I will remember most about today:

60-DAYS OF SELF-REFLECTIONS

Date: /   /

	Today I Feel:
When I need support, I can count on...	☐ Optimistic
	☐ Happy
I felt inspired when...	☐ Uneasy
	☐ Frustrated
I felt happiest when...	☐ Lonely
	☐ Angry
	☐ Tired

I am grateful for...

I felt disrespected/stressed when...

I spoke up when...

I could have done this better...

I know I'm the "man" when...

This was hard but I overcame it by...

I will relax and indulge in self-care today by...

This is what I will remember most about today:

60-DAYS OF SELF-REFLECTIONS

Date: /   /

When I need support, I can count on...	**Today I Feel:**
	☐ Optimistic
	☐ Happy
I felt inspired when...	☐ Uneasy
	☐ Frustrated
	☐ Lonely
I felt happiest when...	☐ Angry
	☐ Tired

I am grateful for...

I felt disrespected/stressed when...

I spoke up when...

I could have done this better...

I know I'm the "man" when...

This was hard but I overcame it by...

I will relax and indulge in self-care today by...

This is what I will remember most about today:

60-DAYS OF SELF-REFLECTIONS

Date: /   /

When I need support, I can count on...	**Today I Feel:**
	☐ Optimistic
I felt inspired when...	☐ Happy
	☐ Uneasy
	☐ Frustrated
I felt happiest when...	☐ Lonely
	☐ Angry
	☐ Tired

I am grateful for...

I felt disrespected/stressed when...

I spoke up when...

I could have done this better...

I know I'm the "man" when...

This was hard but I overcame it by...

I will relax and indulge in self-care today by...

This is what I will remember most about today:

60-DAYS OF SELF-REFLECTIONS

Date: /   /

When I need support, I can count on...	**Today I Feel:** ☐ Optimistic ☐ Happy
I felt inspired when...	☐ Uneasy ☐ Frustrated ☐ Lonely
I felt happiest when...	☐ Angry ☐ Tired

I am grateful for...

I felt disrespected/stressed when...

I spoke up when...

I could have done this better...

I know I'm the "man" when...

This was hard but I overcame it by...

I will relax and indulge in self-care today by...

This is what I will remember most about today:

60-DAYS OF SELF-REFLECTIONS

Date: /   /

When I need support, I can count on...	**Today I Feel:** ☐ Optimistic ☐ Happy
I felt inspired when...	☐ Uneasy ☐ Frustrated
I felt happiest when...	☐ Lonely ☐ Angry ☐ Tired

I am grateful for...

I felt disrespected/stressed when...

I spoke up when...

I could have done this better...

I know I'm the "man" when...

This was hard but I overcame it by...

I will relax and indulge in self-care today by...

This is what I will remember most about today:

60-DAYS OF SELF-REFLECTIONS

Date: /   /

	Today I Feel:
When I need support, I can count on...	☐ Optimistic
	☐ Happy
I felt inspired when...	☐ Uneasy
	☐ Frustrated
	☐ Lonely
I felt happiest when...	☐ Angry
	☐ Tired

I am grateful for...

I felt disrespected/stressed when...

I spoke up when...

I could have done this better...

I know I'm the "man" when...

This was hard but I overcame it by...

I will relax and indulge in self-care today by...

This is what I will remember most about today:

OTHER GUIDED JOURNALS & DIARIES *by* KINYATTA E. GRAY

I Miss You...

Daily Writing Prompts for Reflection, Remembrance, and Spirit Renewal

My Life My Love My Truth

LGBTQ journal

Fashionista's Travel Diary

A Guided Travel Diary for Travel Planning & Reflections

Sexy Baby Mama

Self-Love | Self-Reflections | Spirit Renewal

I'm Doing Me

The Ultimate Breakup Diary for Venting, Reflection & Spirit Renewal

The "Hallelujah" Notes

While I'm Still Here

A Guided Expression Journal of Life, Love and Legacy for Those Preparing to Transition

Caring for Every Inch of Me

Daily Reflections for Self-Care & Spirit Renewal

My Crazy Teenage Life

The Ultimate Expression Diary for Venting, Self-Reflections and Self-Love

Chapter 30

Capturing Life, Love & Lessons in my 30s

I Am A Man. I Have Feelings.

A Guided 90-Day Self-Reflections & Gratitude Journal for Men

Chapter 40

Capturing Life, Love & Lessons in my 40s

The Queen's Manifestation Journal

Daily Writing Prompt for Manifesting the Life You Want

Chapter 50

Capturing Life, Love & Lessons in my 50s

Budget & Shop

A Monthly Personal Budget & Expense Tracker for Young Adults

Remembering Mom

A Grief Journal for Reflections and Remembrance

Kinyatta E. Gray is a Best-Selling Author, Travel Influencer and the CEO of FlightsInStilettos, LLC.

Websites:

https://www.flightsinstilettos.com/

https://www.etsy.com/shop/StylishWritingCenter

Disclaimer:
Kinyatta Gray is not a mental health provider and is providing this information based on her personal experiences. If you are experiencing an emotional crisis, seek the help of a professional mental health provider immediately.

www.ingramcontent.com/pod-product-compliance
Lightning Source LLC
Chambersburg PA
CBHW070439130626

46553CB00006B/2258